FIESTA!

INDIA

GROLIER EDUCATIONAL
SHERMAN TURNPIKE, DANBURY, CONNECTICUT 06816

Published 1997 by Grolier Educational
Sherman Turnpike, Danbury, Connecticut.
Copyright © 1997 Marshall Cavendish Limited.

Set ISBN : 0-7172-9099-9
Volume ISBN : 0-7172-9108-1

Library of Congress Cataloging-in-Publication Data
India.
p.cm. -- (Fiesta! (Danbury, Conn.)
Includes index.
Summary: Discusses the festivals of India and how their songs, recipes, and traditions
reflect the culture of the people.
ISBN 0-7172-9108-1 (hardbound)
1. Festivals -- India -- Juvenile literature. 2. India -- Social life and customs -- Juvenile literature. [1. Festivals --
India. 2. Holidays -- India. 3. India -- Social life and customs.]
I. Series: Fiesta! (Danbury, Conn.)
GT4876.A2148 1997
394.26954--DC21
97-5241
CIP
AC

Marshall Cavendish Limited
Editorial staff
Editorial Director: Ellen Dupont
Series Designer: Joyce Mason
Crafts devised and created by Susan Moxley
Music arrangements by Harry Boteler
Photographs by Bruce Mackie
Subeditors: Susan Janes, Judy Fovargue
Production: Craig Chubb

For this volume
Editor: Susie Dawson
Designer: Trevor Vertigan
Consultant: V.P. (Hemant) Kanitkar
Editorial Assistant: Bindu Mathur

Printed in Italy

Adult supervision advised for all crafts and recipes
particularly those involving sharp instruments and heat.

CONTENTS

INDIA:

India has a huge range of landscapes. In the north are the highest mountains in the world. It also has deserts and tropical jungles.

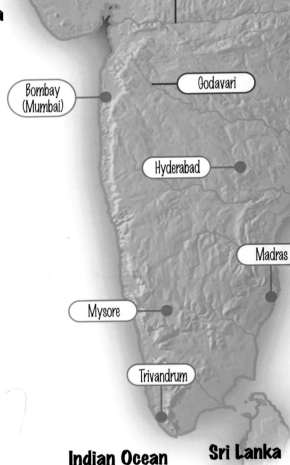

Himala...

Indus

Jaipur

DELHI

Pakistan

Udaipur

Narmada

Arabian Sea

Godavari

Bombay (Mumbai)

Hyderabad

Madras

Mysore

Trivandrum

Indian Ocean　　**Sri Lanka**

▼ **The Taj Mahal** is one of the most beautiful buildings in the world. It was built as a tomb and is 350 years old.

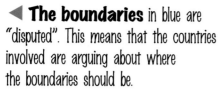 **The boundaries** in blue are "disputed". This means that the countries involved are arguing about where the boundaries should be.

Nepal

Ganga

China

Bhutan

aranasi

Bangladesh

Myanmar (Burma)

ndia

Calcutta

Bay of Bengal

Puri

▲ **The India Gate** stands over the main road of Delhi, the capital of India. The capital was moved here by the British early in the 20th century.

◄ **Shiva** is often shown in statues as Lord of the Dance. He is one of the main gods of the Hindu religion. Most Indians are Hindus.

▲ **Spices** of all different colors and flavors are used in Indian cooking. As well as tasting delicious, they help to preserve the food longer in India's hot climate.

5

RELIGIONS

Religion plays an important part in people's lives in India. Most people follow the Hindu religion, but there are also people from all the other important religions in the world.

HINDUISM is the major religion of India. About eight people out of every ten are Hindus. It is one of the oldest religions in the world. Hindus believe that a person's soul is born again, after death, into another body. This rebirth is called reincarnation. They also believe God has many different forms. Some of these are male, and some are female. Each of these gods and goddesses has its own personality, and Hindus pray to them for different things. Hindus give thanks to their gods at festivals throughout the year. The dates for these festivals are based on the movements of the moon, and so they do not occur on the same day every year.

ISLAM is a religion that comes from the Middle East. It spread to India when trading first started between the two areas. Islam is the second largest religion in India. Followers of Islam are called Muslims. Muslims believe in one God whom they call Allah. His word was made known to man through the prophet Mohammed. His teachings are written down in the Muslim holy book, the *Koran*.

BUDDHISM was started in India about 2,500 years ago by a man who became known as the Buddha, or enlightened one. This means that he was very wise and understood all things. The festivals of Buddhism celebrate the major events in the Buddha's life. Although Buddhism started in India, there are not many Buddhists in India now.

SIKHISM is the religion of the Sikhs, a word that means disciples. Most Sikhs live in the northwest of India. It was here about 500 years ago that the religion was started by a man called Guru Nanak. *Guru* means teacher. Sikhs believe in one God. Their temple is called a *gurdwara*, and it is here that their holy book, the *Guru Granth Sahib*, is kept. They celebrate many of the same festivals as the Hindus.

CHRISTIANITY has about 20 million followers. It was brought to India in the 16th century by Portuguese traders. Most of the Christians in India are Roman Catholics.

JAINISM is based on the teachings of a man who lived at the same time as the Buddha. Jains are strict vegetarians. They try not to injure any living thing. The monks even wear veils over their noses and mouths so as not to breathe in an insect and kill it.

Greetings From **INDIA!**

India is a big country with over 900 million people. Not everyone in India is the same. The people in different parts of the country look different, have different customs, and speak different languages.

There are 18 official languages as well as hundreds of dialects. Indians from different parts of the country can often only talk to each other in English. Hindi is spoken more than any other language, but still only one in five Indians speaks it. The expressions given here are in Hindi.

When Indians meet each other, they don't shake hands. Instead they put their palms together and bow their heads slightly. The garment shown here is worn by Indian women and is called a sari.

How do you say...

Hello
Namaste
Goodbye
Acchaa
Thank you
Dhanya vaad
Peace
Shanti

PONGAL HARVEST FESTIVAL

This festival is celebrated in the south of India in January. Rice is the main crop in this area. Pongal is a festival of thanksgiving for the harvest of the winter rice.

Pongal happens over three main days. On the first day people clean their houses. They burn the garbage on huge bonfires. Everyone spends the evening around the fires. Young children bang drums as hard as they can.

The main part of the second day is the worship of Surya, the sun god who helped to ripen the rice. A kind of rice pudding is offered to Surya and then given to the family to eat. The common greeting on

All cattle are sacred to Hindus. Cows are honored for the milk they give and oxen for the work they do in the fields.

PONGAL RICE

SERVES 4 TO 6

¾ cup short-grained rice
1½ cups water
2 quarts milk
4 green cardamom pods
1¼ cups sugar
¼ tsp ground cardamom (optional)
1 tbsp rose water
¼ cup chopped pistachio nuts

1 Put rice in saucepan with the water and bring to a boil over high heat. Simmer 5 minutes. Drain.
2 In large, heavy bottomed pan, bring milk and cardamom pods to a boil. Add rice and simmer slowly, stirring occasionally, for 1 hour, or until rice is very soft. Stir in sugar. Continue simmering until mixture is stiff.
3 Remove pan from heat. Use a spoon to remove cardamom pods. Taste pudding and, if you think it needs more flavor, stir in ground cardamom. Let cool to lukewarm. Stir in rose water and nuts.
4 Decorate with unsprayed rose petals. Serve warm or chilled.

this day is "Paal pongrita?" which means "Has the milk boiled over?" The boiling over of milk with rice is symbolic of wealth and prosperity. The word "pongal" means "overflowing."

The third day is the day when people worship cattle. Cattle are considered special in India. Hindus do not eat beef. In some states it is against the law to kill cattle at all.

During Pongal the cattle are thanked for their work plowing the land. They are washed and decorated with flower garlands. Then the cattle eat rice pudding too!

GARLANDS

Brightly colored flowers sewn together in garlands are a common sight at any festival or celebration. They are used by Muslims, Sikhs, and Buddhists as well as by Hindus. Putting flower garlands around someone's neck is a sign of great honor and respect. At Pongal respect for cattle is shown in this way.

The garlands shown here have been made from tissue paper. The ones used in India, however, are made from real flowers.

HOLI FESTIVAL

Everyone has fun at the Hindu spring festival of Holi. It happens in March, lasts for two days, and is known as the festival of color.

Holi begins with the lighting of a big bonfire by a priest. This is the signal for all the other fires in the area to be lighted. The story of Holi is based around a wicked female demon called Holika who ends up being destroyed in a fire. Images of her are put on top of the bonfires and are burned. Small coins are thrown into the fire, and coconuts are roasted around the edge of it. People put ashes from the fire on their foreheads to bring happiness in the year ahead.

The next morning people make sure to wear their old clothes.

A brightly colored box is decorated with dancing women.

Dances with sticks are performed at Holi and other festivals. Each dancer holds a stick and strikes it at right angles against another dancer's stick. The sticks may be brightly painted or ribboned.

On this day people throw colored paints, powders, or water at each other. Old or young, rich or poor, no one is spared. It is

10

THE CASTE SYSTEM

The caste system in India is a kind of class system linked to Hinduism. Caste is inherited from the family you are born in and cannot be changed. Caste used to dictate the job you did.

Brahmins are the highest caste. In past times nearly all priests and scholars were Brahmins. The lowest caste were known as the Untouchables. They had to do the dirtiest jobs, like sweeping the streets. Since 1950 the whole idea of "Untouchability" has become illegal. Nowadays you can do any job you choose, and the caste you belong to is not so important.

It is only important now for marriage. Most people marry someone who is from the same caste.

These instruments are used to make music at festival times.

considered good luck to get splattered in this way. Everyone has fun, and the streets are full of noise and excitement.

In the past it was a time when caste was forgotten for a day. The lowliest sweeper could throw paint on the richest landlord without fear of punishment.

BAISAKHI

On April 13, the date of Baisakhi, people who belong to the Sikh religion celebrate their New Year and commemorate the birth of their brotherhood.

Baisakhi is a time when Sikhs remember all the promises they made when they joined the brotherhood of Sikhs. It is also a time when new members join the religion. As they join, they are baptized with a sweet water known as *amrit*. They agree to take a new name. All Sikh men become known as *Singh*, which means lion, and all Sikh women take the name of *Kaur*, which means princess.

Before the ceremony there are prayers and readings from the holy book, the *Granth Sahib*. After it everyone eats a vegetarian meal in a special room in the temple.

SIKH FLAG

A triangular yellow flag flies above every Sikh temple. At Baisakhi there is a short ceremony when the old one is taken down, the flag post is washed, and a new flag is put in its place.

The black design on the flag is the symbol of the Sikh religion. It has a black circle with a double-edged sword through its center. There are crossed daggers around the edge.

The kirpan (dagger), kangha (comb), and kara (bangle) are three of the five "Ks" that Sikhs must wear. The other two are kesh (uncut hair) and kachara (special underpants).

The ten leaders, or gurus, of the Sikh religion throughout its history.

RAKSHA BANDHAN

Raksha Bandhan is celebrated by most Hindu and Sikh families. On this day in July or August sisters tie braided bracelets, called rakhis, round the wrists of their brothers.

Before the festival girls choose the *rakhis* they will give to their brothers.

On the day itself the sister marks her brother's forehead with a red powder, called *kum kum*, and then ties the rakhi on her brother's right wrist. As she does this, she wishes him happiness and success in all he does. In return he pledges to guard and protect her with his life. She then puts a candy in his mouth.

In this way sisters show their love for their brothers. Girls who have no brothers may perform the ceremony with a cousin or friend.

ALMOND BURFI

MAKES 30 PIECES
½ cup sugar
½ cup water
2 cups blanched almonds
⅔ cup milk
1 can (14 oz) sweetened condensed milk
1½ sticks butter, cut up
silver leaf or colored sugar
¼ cup chopped pistachio nuts

1 Grease an 8 x 10 in baking pan; set aside. Have an adult put sugar and water in pan over low heat. Stir to dissolve sugar.

Put candy thermometer in pan.
2 Boil 10 minutes, or until syrup reaches 234° to 240° F, or when a small amount dropped in ice-cold water forms a soft ball.
3 Meanwhile, put almonds and 4 tbsp milk in a blender. Blend until rough paste forms. Add remaining milk and blend again.
4 Stir almond paste, butter, and condensed milk into syrup. Boil, stirring often, 30 to 40 minutes until it

reaches 234° to 240° F again.
5 Pour into pan and spread out evenly. Lay silver leaf over half or sprinkle with sugar. Scatter nuts over half. Chill overnight to set. To serve, cut into squares.

RAKHI BRACELETS

YOU WILL NEED
Thin colored cardboard
Large buttons
Assorted sequins
Colored ribbons

3 Now glue the decorated cardboard onto the button. To make the strap, cut three lengths of ribbon roughly two and a half times the length of braid you want to make. Knot them together at one end and braid. Knot the other ends of the ribbons together. Tie the thin ribbon around the strap, and your rakhi is ready to wear.

1 Choose a fairly large round button. Cut a circle of cardboard the same size as the button. Decorate the top of the cardboard by gluing an assortment of colored sequins onto it.

2 Sew a thin piece of ribbon through the holes in the button. You will use this ribbon to attach the button to the strap of the rakhi.

JANMASHTAMI – KRISHNA'S BIRTHDAY

Krishna is one of the most popular Hindu gods, so his birthday in the month of August is celebrated with great fondness and joy.

Krishna was one of the forms in which the god Vishnu appeared on earth to protect people from evil.

For the celebration of Krishna's birthday, many Hindus stay up all night at temples watching scenes from his life being acted out. At midnight, a statue of Krishna is washed with a mixture of clarified butter, called *ghee*, milk, sugar, and honey. This mix is then shared out among everyone. A statue of the baby Krishna is placed in a decorated cradle or swing, and everyone takes turns rocking it.

This brass statue shows Krishna as a crawling baby.

Fish

Tortoise

Boar

Man-Lion

HARI KRISHNA

This song honors two Hindu gods, Krishna in the first verse and Rama in the second. They are both forms, or incarnations, of the god Vishnu. In the song Vishnu is referred to as Hari. The music is usually repeated again and again, getting faster the more it is repeated.

Ha - ri   Krish - na ———   Ha - ri   Krish - na ———

— Krish - na   Krish - na ———   Ha - ri   ha - ri. ———

Hari Rama Hari Rama
Rama Rama Hari Hari.

The figures below show nine of the different forms in which Vishnu appears on earth. The other one is Krishna (above).

Dwarf

Parashurama

Rama

Buddha

Rider on white horse

17

THE BIRTH OF KRISHNA

On the festival of Krishna's birthday the story of his birth is read out loud in temples and homes. Krishna is a popular Hindu god, and the dramatic story of his narrow escape from death on the day of his birth is well-known to Hindu children.

THE KING OF MATHURA had a son called Kamsa and a daughter named Devaki. Kamsa was evil. He decided to put his father in prison and rule in his place.

Devaki married Prince Vasudeva. On the day of their wedding Kamsa heard a heavenly voice saying that he would be killed by one of their children. Kamsa immediately put Devaki and Vasudeva in prison where he kept them for many years.

Each child that Devaki bore was killed as soon as it was born. When Devaki was pregnant for the eighth time, Kamsa again ordered everyone to be vigilant. At midnight one dark and stormy night Devaki's eighth child was born. This time it was the god Krishna. The baby immediately took on the form of a grownup, revealing himself to Prince Vasudeva as an incarnation of the god Vishnu. He told Vasudeva how to get him safely out of prison.

After Krishna had become a baby again, Vasudeva put him in a basket and covered him to keep him warm. As he walked toward the prison gates, the locks fell away, and the doors opened on their own. The guards were sound asleep as he stepped over them to get out. Vasudeva walked out into the stormy night, and as he approached the Yamuna River, its waters divided, allowing him to cross

over. He went to the house of a cowherd, Nanda. Nanda's wife had given birth to a daughter just that day. Vasudeva left his baby son there and took the baby girl back to the prison with him. He was able to walk back in just as he had walked out.

Once Vasudeva and the baby were back inside the cell, the guards woke up. They called Kamsa to tell him that the baby had been born. Kamsa came to the prison and snatched the baby girl. The girl was also a divine being. She rose up out of his arms. Then she told him that the real child of Vasudeva and Devaki was safely out of his reach on the other side of the river. She promised that the child, a boy named Krishna, would grow up to kill him, and Krishna did just that!

GANESHA FESTIVAL

The elephant-headed god, Ganesha, is worshipped throughout India, but he is most popular in the city of Bombay (Mumbai). His festival is celebrated privately in homes as well as in street processions.

In the days leading up to the Ganesha festival there is much excitement as children go from shop to shop to choose their favorite Ganesha statue. The statues are usually made of clay. The god has an elephant's head and four arms.

The statue is brought home and put up in a specially decorated place. Gifts are given to it, and for as long as the festival lasts, the image is thought to possess the spirit of the god.

During the public celebrations everyone gathers to worship a much larger image of the god. On the last day this is paraded through the streets and thrown into the local river.

It is thought that Ganesha helps things go smoothly. He is worshipped at the start of any new project.

HOW GANESHA GOT HIS ELEPHANT HEAD

THE GODDESS PARVATI used to get bored while her husband Shiva was away from home. One day she made a baby boy out of clay. When she dried it in the sun, it came alive.

When Shiva came home and found a small boy in his house, he got jealous and chopped off the boy's head. Parvati was very upset and made Shiva replace the head with the head of the first creature he could find. Since this was an elephant, Ganesha got an elephant's head. He has had it ever since.

Various gifts have been laid out in front of Ganesha's statue. They include some of his favorite things — candy and fruit to satisfy his huge appetite, and flowers and incense to please his sense of smell.

NAVRATRI AND DASARA

These festivals honor the mother goddess. Together they last for ten days and are held every year in September or October.

Navratri means "nine nights," and Dasara means "tenth day." Navratri comes just before Dasara, and together they make up a ten-day festival that celebrates the mother goddess. She is known as Durga in some parts of India. This part of the year is a time of rest for the people who work on the land. The hard farming work is over.

The main way of celebrating is dancing around the shrine of the goddess. Dasara, the tenth day, is the most special. On this day children are not shouted at even if they are bad. It is good luck to start something on the day of

The goddess Durga holds the weapons she used to defeat the buffalo demon. In Hindu mythology she rides a lion. The animal in this carving looks more like a tiger.

Dasara. Children may be taught the alphabet for the first time. Grownups try to start a new business or to buy a new house on this day.

In eastern India the festival celebrates the victory of Durga over a buffalo demon who wanted to destroy the world.

Hindus think that the goddess comes down to earth for the ten days of the festival. It is a time of great celebration, especially for women. Married women go home to visit their families. Decorated statues of Durga are made up. People offer flowers and incense to the goddess. On the last day the images are put into the river. People are sad when she goes, but she will be back next year.

In the city of Mysore there is a famous procession of elephants during the festival.

THE RAMAYANA

People in the north of India celebrate this festival by acting out a famous Hindu legend called the Ramayana. The story tells the adventures of Prince Rama in his battle to overthrow the evil King Ravana. With the help of the monkey god, Hanuman, Rama eventually defeats Ravana. The festival often ends with huge models of Ravana being blown up. The shadow puppet shown here is Hanuman. It is made of leather. It is used in puppet shows that tell the story of the Ramayana.

THE RESCUE OF PRINCESS SITA

Episodes from the Hindu poem the Ramayana are acted out at the festival of Navratri and Dasara. The Ramayana tells the story of Prince Rama. It tells how he won his wife Sita's hand in marriage and of his adventures during 14 years of exile. During this time he rescues his wife from a wicked demon king called Ravana.

PRINCE RAMA was the eldest son and heir of King Dasharatha, who ruled a kingdom in northern India. Rama's best friend was his brother Lakshman. Prince Rama was a skilled archer. He won the hand of his beautiful wife, Princess Sita, in an archery contest.

King Dasharatha's youngest wife was jealous of Rama. She tricked her husband into exiling his son and making her son heir instead. Rama sadly left home with Lakshman and Sita.

While in exile the three lived in a forest. One day, when Rama and Lakshman were out hunting, Sita was kidnapped by the wicked King Ravana, a demon with ten heads. The two princes searched for her for many months. They were helped by a monkey general whose name was Hanuman.

At last Hanuman found Sita in Ravana's kingdom of Lanka. Hanuman gave Sita a ring from Rama and told her she would soon be rescued.

But Hanuman was captured and brought before King Ravana. As a punishment Ravana ordered that the monkey's tail was to be set alight. But Hanuman was smart. He stretched out his tail and set fire to half Ravana's capital city. Then he escaped and returned to Rama.

Rama decided to attack Lanka to rescue Sita. Hanuman organized an army of monkeys to help. After crossing the ocean, he led his soldiers to

Ravana's capital. Ravana refused to release Sita. During the battles that followed, Lakshman was seriously wounded. The doctor said he could only cure the wounds if he had four healing herbs from a certain mountain.

Hanuman rushed to fetch them, but when he reached the mountain, he didn't know which herbs the doctor wanted. So he uprooted the whole mountain and took it to Lanka. Lakshman was saved.

In the final battle between Rama and Ravana, Rama used the god Indra's dart to pierce Ravana's heart. The king of Lanka fell down dead. At last Rama was reunited with Sita.

Then Rama, Sita, Lakshman, and Hanuman returned home in a flying carriage. The people of the capital were delighted to welcome them after their victory. Banners and flags hung from the houses and decorated the streets. At night the city glittered with hundreds of tiny lamps that had been put out to light their way home.

DIVALI

This festival celebrates the new year for businesses. It happens in the autumn and is known as the festival of lights. Little clay lamps or "divas" are lighted in every home.

This festival is held in honor of Lakshmi, the Hindu goddess of wealth and prosperity. It is treated as the beginning of the new year for businesses. All debts should be paid, and new account books are started.

Divas are lighted and placed in windows or outside the house. Where rivers are nearby, small boats made

To shape this diva, cut the clay out into the leaf shape while still flat. Then bend up the edges and use your finger to make the pattern on the rim.

MAKING DIVAS

Since Divali is the festival of light, it is a good idea to make as many divas as you can in as many shapes as you can. Use a modeling clay that is self-hardening, and shape your diva as you like. Allow enough room for a night-light candle to go inside. Build the clay up gradually, and moisten the edges when you put two pieces together to make sure they stick. Leave to dry. Decorate your diva using nonflammable paints. When the paint is dry, glue on ribbons and sequins.

RANGOLI PATTERNS

At important festivals like Divali women decorate their homes and temples by drawing patterns on the ground outside. They draw these designs with a mixture of rice flour and water. Colored powders may also be used. These designs provide a cheap but very effective form of decoration.

You can try this out yourself with powder paints or glitter. Special designs are sometimes used for a particular occasion, but any pattern will do. It can be geometric or in the form of a fruit, flower, leaf, or religious symbol.

Get a piece of cardboard or stiff paper. Paint it all over with one color. A dark color is a good idea if you want to use white powder on top. Mark out your design lightly in pencil. Paint over the design with glue, then carefully sprinkle the colored powder on top. When dry, tip up the paper, and any surplus powder will fall off.

During the festival people light hundreds of lamps, or divas. The more lamps people light, the more likely it is that Lakshmi will be tempted to visit them. Hindus believe that the goddess brings her wealth with her when she visits.

of leaves or coconut shells are used to carry divas downstream and out to sea.

Visits are made to relatives and friends. Food is shared, and trays of candy are given as presents. Greeting cards are sent. Houses are cleaned up and decorated. People dress in new clothes and take food offerings to their local temple.

EID-UL-FITR –
A MUSLIM FESTIVAL

This Muslim festival comes at a different time every year depending on the phases of the moon. It marks the end of the month of Ramadan, when Muslims fast and pray.

The coming of Eid-ul-Fitr is a time of celebration for all Muslims everywhere. It comes at the end of a month of fasting and prayers. "Eid-ul-Fitr" means "Feast of the Breaking of the Fast." Houses are cleaned and decorated in preparation. The month of fasting begins on seeing the new moon and ends on seeing the next new moon.

Fireworks are set off to show that Eid has arrived. If the sky

As part of Eid delicate patterns are painted onto the palms of women's hands. These patterns are painted with paste made from the henna plant. The paste dyes the hand a rich golden-red color. It stays on the hands for two or three weeks. The patterns are sometimes put on with the help of stencils like the two shown here.

28

EID SONG

This song is sung throughout the Muslim world. The words are in Arabic. It is sung for Mohammed's birthday as well as for Eid.

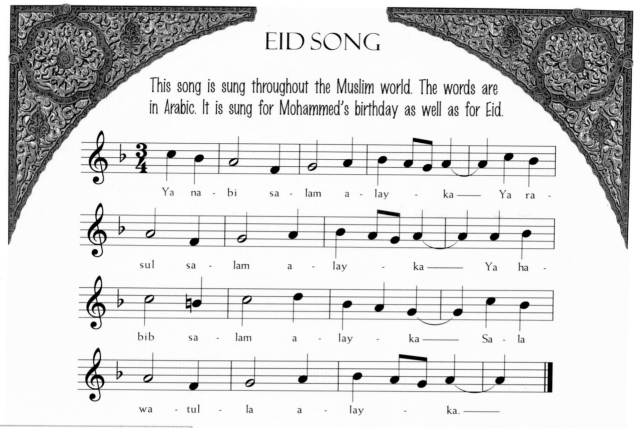

Ya na - bi sa - lam a - lay - ka —— Ya ra -

sul sa - lam a - lay - ka —— Ya ha -

bib sa - lam a - lay - ka —— Sa - la

wa - tul - la a - lay - ka. ——

Oh prophet, peace be upon you,
Oh messenger, peace be upon you,
Oh beloved, peace be upon you,
Prayers of Allah upon you.

is overcast that night and the moon cannot be seen, then the start of Eid is postponed by 24 hours.

True Eid starts the following morning. Everyone goes to the mosque for prayers. They greet each other with the words "Eid Mubarak." Older relatives give gifts of money to younger ones. This gift of money is known as *eidee*. Everyone tries to visit their relatives and visitors are given candies and desserts. Because this is the end of a month of fasting a lot of delicious food is prepared and eaten.

RAMADAN

The Muslim year is based on lunar months. During the ninth month, known as Ramadan, Muslims fast from sunrise to sunset. They do not eat or drink anything during these hours. In the evening they break their fast with a few dates or some other fruit.

OTHER FESTIVALS

PUSHKAR MELA Pushkar is a small town in the desert area of northwest India. In November every year thousands of people arrive for the *mela*, or fair. A city of tents grows up in the desert. The fair is a chance to buy and sell animals as well as other goods. There is a fairground with a Ferris wheel and sideshows as well as entertainers. Jugglers, snake charmers, and acrobats all perform.

Many of the animals traded at the Pushkar Mela are camels. There are also cattle and horses for sale.

REPUBLIC DAY On January 26 every year India celebrates the day in 1950 when it became a republic. The biggest celebration is in New Delhi, where there is a huge display of soldiers, tanks, and airplanes. There are also decorated floats, musicians, and folk dancers.

This brightly colored hanging is a decoration for any festive occasion.

RATH YATRA At the end of June in the town of Puri on the east coast of India there is one of the most spectacular festivals of the year. It is held in honor of the god Jagannath. The main event of the festival is the procession of three huge chariots pulled by thousands of pilgrims. The chariots are about 45 feet high, with wheels at least six feet in diameter.

The word "Juggernaut," which means a huge war machine, comes from the word Jagannath.

This small wooden box contains images of Lord Jagannath and his brother and sister. They are the three gods pulled through the streets for the Rath Yatra festival.

WORDS TO KNOW

Caste system: This Indian class system used to determine the jobs that people did. It is based on ancient Hindu scriptures that split society into four groups: priests, warriors, merchants and farmers, and laborers. Over the centuries, these main groups were split into hundreds of smaller castes. Below all the castes were the outcastes, or Untouchables.

Dialect: A regional variety of a language.

Fast: To go without food deliberately.

Guru: A spiritual teacher or guide.

Incense: A mixture of gum and spice that gives off a pleasing smell when burned. Incense is often used in religious services.

Lunar calendar: In this calendar a month is the time between two new moons — about 29 days. Muslim, Buddhist, and Hindu festivals are based on this calendar.

Mosque: A place of worship for Muslims.

Pilgrim: A person who makes a religious journey, or pilgrimage, to a holy place.

Ramadan: The ninth month of the Muslim year, during which Muslims fast from dawn until sunset.

Reincarnation: The Hindu belief that people are reborn into different bodies after they die. If a person has been good, they will be more successful in their next life. If they have been bad, they will be reborn into a lower caste, or even as an animal.

Republic: A country whose head of state is not a king or queen but a leader who has been elected by the people.

Shrine: A place set aside for the worship of gods and goddesses. Most Hindu worship takes place in front of shrines set up in the home.

Temple: A place of worship. Hindus, Buddhists, and Sikhs worship at temples.

Vegetarian: A person who does not eat meat.

ACKNOWLEDGMENTS

WITH THANKS TO:

Articles of Faith, Religious Artefacts and Resources for Education, Bury, Lancashire. Fifth Dimension, London. Ganesha Textiles, London. Religion in Evidence, Alfreton, Derbyshire. Shri Sai Temple, London. So High Soho, London. Soma Folk Traditions of India, London.

PHOTOGRAPHS BY:

All photographs by Bruce Mackie.
Cover photograph Robert Harding Picture Library.

ILLUSTRATIONS BY:

Fiona Saunders title page p4-5, Mountain High Maps ® Copyright © 1993 Digital Wisdom, Inc. p4-5. Tracy Rich p7. Josephine Martin p19.

SET CONTENTS